THE WEDDING OF
HARRY & MEGHAN

Souvenir Programme

St George's Chapel, Windsor Castle
Saturday, 19 May 2018

© REGAL PRESS LIMITED

Printed in the UK by Severnprint Limited on 115g Chorus Silk. This paper has been independently certified according to the standards of the Forest Stewardship Council® (FSC)®.

ISBN: 978-1-906670-67-2

His Royal Highness The Prince of Wales, K.G., K.T.

requests the pleasure of the company of

....

at the Marriage of

His Royal Highness Prince Henry of Wales

with

Ms Meghan Markle

at St. George's Chapel, Windsor Castle

on Saturday, 19th May, 2018 at 12 Noon

followed by a Reception at Windsor Castle

Dress:

A reply is requested to:
The Comptroller, Lord Chamberlain's Office,
Buckingham Palace, London SW1A 1AA

INTRODUCTION

BY ROBERT JOBSON

The genius of a royal wedding lies in the combination of its simplicity, its invocation of history and its sense of splendour. It lies, too, in its ability to appeal to people on a personal level, as well as being a sensational, almost magical, visual spectacle. The build-up to the wedding of Prince Henry of Wales – now sixth in line to the British throne and known popularly as Prince Harry – and his American bride Ms Rachel Meghan Markle has certainly captured the popular imagination.

Celebrated by close friends, family and dedicated royal fans in Windsor, it will be enthusiastically cheered across the country, the Commonwealth and the rest of the world.

This royal wedding – due to be watched by an anticipated global television audience of two billion – as well as being a celebration of love, will bolster Britain's coffers by an estimated £500 million, experts claim.

Harry and Meghan's love story has also given the Royal Family's popularity a huge boost. Not since the days of the late Diana, Princess of Wales, has there been this degree of interest from young people in the Royal Family and the new "princess" who is marrying into it.

Harry, who I've watched grow up while chronicling the Windsor story for more than 25 years, has developed from a mischievous young man into the more mature version of himself we see now. Today, he is a prince who takes his public duties and charity responsibilities very seriously – even if he doesn't appear to take himself too seriously.

In his choice of wife – the beautiful, biracial, divorced actress Meghan – he has once again shown the determination to live his life his way and on his terms. When he met Meghan, he said the "stars were aligned". She was "the one" and he said he knew he would have to "raise his game" to woo her. Their modern-day love story may not be the stuff of fairy tales, but it is an enchanting love story of our times.

This book, published by SJH Publishing, is a celebration in photographs and words of Harry and Meghan's love story. Using the brilliant images of my friend Robin Nunn – whose firm Nunn Syndication is the world's largest independently owned specialist royal photographic image source – the book captures the very essence of these two people as it documents their journey together and their historic union.

Harry is truly a prince for our times. Together with Meghan he has helped the Royal Family show itself to be much more in touch with the public it serves. And his princely marriage has the power to unite us all.

I am sure you will want to join me in raising a glass and wishing Prince Harry and Meghan Markle all the happiness in the world on their future life together.

CONTENTS

Chapter One

THE WEDDING

The union of Harry and Meghan
looks set to be a unique transatlantic
celebration – even if they are trying to
keep the occasion relatively low key –
with a lot of personal touches from
the glamorous bride and groom

It has all the hallmarks of the grand finale of a Hollywood love story, only this romantic tale stars a real-life prince, Henry of Wales, and his beautiful actress Meghan Markle.

This showpiece wedding, with the historic Windsor Castle as its backdrop, will attract an audience of millions from around the world, too. Imbued with centuries-old tradition, it will feature British pomp and pageantry at its finest, all staged in the majestic St George's Chapel of Windsor Castle, the final resting place of ancient English kings and queens, and the setting for centuries of royal history.

With two little words, "I will", the beautiful American-born bride Ms Markle will send cheers ringing around the Berkshire town, where a throng of thousands will stand beyond the castle walls watching the ceremony amid a carnival atmosphere on specially erected big screens. Mingling among them will be media crews from around the world making their final checks on the TV cameras that will overlook Windsor High Street from every possible vantage point in preparation for the moment when the couple emerges through the castle gates in an open carriage.

Inside the Gothic chapel, with its magnificent fan-vaulted ceiling dating back to the reign of Henry VII, the guests, Prince Harry's grandmother Her Majesty The Queen and his father the Prince of Wales will beam with joy as the happy event unfolds.

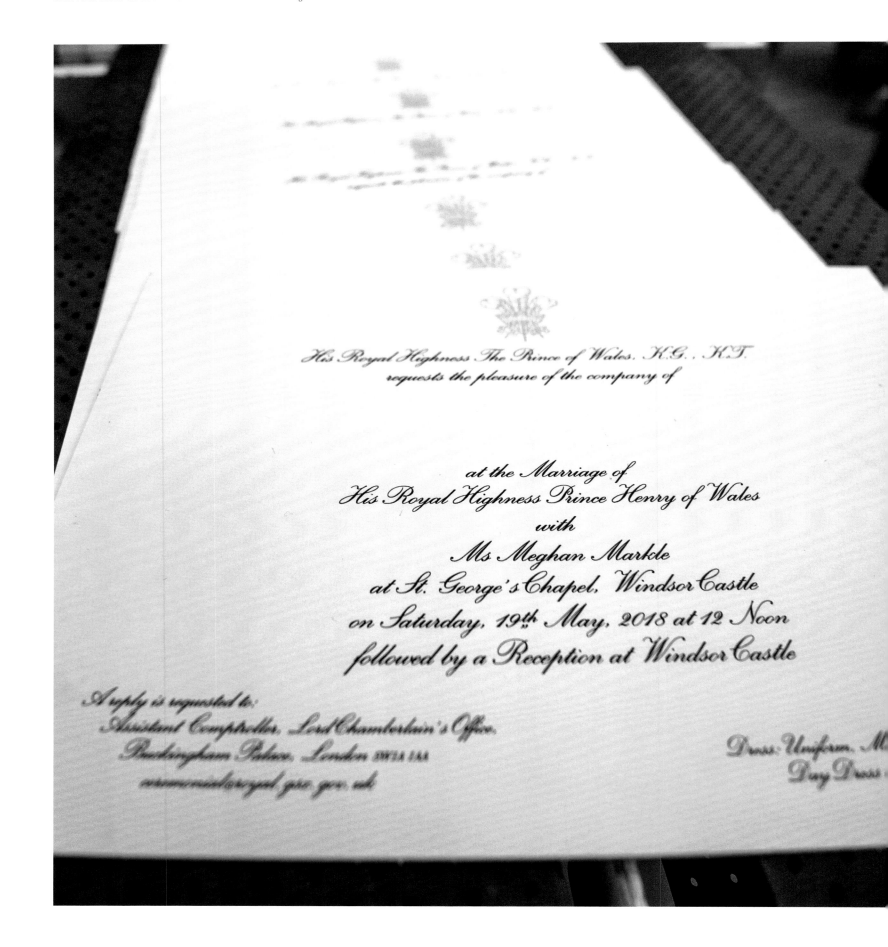

His Royal Highness The Prince of Wales, K.G., K.T.
requests the pleasure of the company of

at the Marriage of
His Royal Highness Prince Henry of Wales
with
Ms Meghan Markle
at St. George's Chapel, Windsor Castle
on Saturday, 19th May, 2018 at 12 Noon
followed by a Reception at Windsor Castle

A reply is requested to:
Assistant Comptroller, Lord Chamberlain's Office,
Buckingham Palace, London SW1A 1AA
ceremonial@royal.gsx.gov.uk

Dress: Uniform, M
Day Dress

It will be one of the major global news events of the year; the hottest ticket in town. But, unlike his brother Prince William's 2011 wedding to Catherine Middleton (later the Duke and Duchess of Cambridge), which took place at Westminster Abbey on 29 April 2011 with 1,900 guests present, this was always going to be a much smaller, more intimate affair.

A REGAL SETTING

Harry and Meghan's venue, St George's Chapel – a Church of England parish within Windsor Castle – has a capacity of only 800 people. From flowers to seating plans, the happy couple will be looking to take charge of their ceremony, which has been designed to embrace those close to them, and also to welcome the public in to enjoy this life-changing moment. Each of the 600 lucky guests invited to the actual wedding – including the Royal Family, Meghan's parents and the couple's friends – will have received a stiff white card sent out in late March, with a select 200 close friends invited to a "VVIP" after-party at Frogmore House, the 17th-century estate just south of Windsor Castle where Harry and Meghan spent time together as their relationship blossomed. The formal burnished gold-and-black invitations with gilded edging, produced by Barnard and Westwood (holder of the Royal Warrant for Printing & Bookbinding by Appointment to Her Majesty The Queen since 1985, as well as one with

"

At the heart of it are two people who have fallen in love with each other, who are committing their lives to each other with the most beautiful words and profound thoughts

"

her heir) were sent from the Prince of Wales for the 19 May noon service at St George's Chapel, Windsor.

However, Harry and Meghan have made it clear that they want to share the wedding with as many members of the public as they can. They have thus invited a further 2,640 lucky members of the general public to Windsor Castle to watch the bride, groom and wedding guests arrive. Buckingham Palace has said that 1,200 members of the public "from every corner of the United Kingdom" will be allowed into the castle grounds, chosen by nine regional Lord Lieutenant offices. The couple wanted these guests to come from a broad range of backgrounds and ages, including young people who have shown strong leadership, and those who have served their communities. It is a nice gesture. A further 200 people from Prince Harry's charities, as well as 100 school pupils, 610 Windsor Castle community members, and 530 members of the Royal Households and Crown Estate have also received the coveted invites.

The couple also wanted to embrace the wider public. Knowing that thousands of people would travel to Windsor to soak up the atmosphere, they have included a carriage ride in an open landau carriage through the streets of Windsor. This tour, their first public appearance as man and wife, will see them being greeted by cheering well-wishers as the carriage makes its way via Castle Hill, along the High Street and through Windsor Town before returning along the Long Walk for their receptions.

It would not be a royal wedding without the involvement of military personnel and the splendour they bring to the occasion. The Queen is Commander-in-Chief of the British Armed Forces and, as sovereign and head of state, is also the Head of the Armed Forces. All military personnel vow "to serve Queen and country".

CEREMONIAL SUPPORT

Regiments and units that hold a special relationship with Prince Harry will provide ceremonial support at the wedding and during the carriage procession at the request of Kensington Palace, with more than 250 members of the Armed Forces performing ceremonial duties. Members of the Household Cavalry will form a staircase party at St George's Chapel, while the State Trumpeters and a Captain's Escort from the Household Cavalry will provide ceremonial support.

Captain Harry Wales – as he was known in the army – joined the Blues and Royals in April 2006 and served with the Household Cavalry Regiment, undertaking two tours of Afghanistan and rising to the rank of Captain. Royal Marines will also be on duty as Harry is Captain General Royal Marines, the ceremonial head of the force, after succeeding the Duke of Edinburgh in the role in December 2017.

There will be personnel from 3 Regiment Army Air Corps on duty too, as Harry served as an Apache pilot in Helmand Province, Afghanistan with 662 Squadron, 3 Regiment Army Air Corps. The Royal Gurkha Rifles will also be present, as Harry served with the 1st Battalion The Royal Gurkha Rifles in Afghanistan in 2007. They will be joined by personnel from RAF Honington, as Harry is Honorary Air Commandant of RAF Honington. Musical support to the street liners will be provided by the Band of the Irish Guards.

Streets within the precincts of Windsor Castle will be lined by members of the Windsor Castle Guard from 1st Battalion the Irish Guards and by Armed Forces personnel from the Royal Navy Small Ships and Diving, as Harry is Commodore-in-Chief, Small Ships and Diving.

"I am proud that members of the Armed Forces have been asked to take part in the ceremonial celebrations taking place on the royal couple's wedding day," said Air Chief Marshal Sir Stuart Peach, Chief of the Defence Staff. "It is a happy occasion for the whole country and reminds us of the role the Armed Forces play in marking important events in the life of the nation. I am particularly pleased to hear that members of the Armed Forces who have a close relationship with Prince Harry will be taking part. Servicemen and women from the Royal Navy, Army and Royal Air Force will all be honoured to offer their support."

Harry and Meghan are delighted that members of the Armed Forces will play such a special role in their wedding. "The military, and these units in particular, hold a great significance for Prince Harry and the couple

are incredibly grateful for their support," said a Kensington Palace spokesperson.

A FAMILY AFFAIR

The core aspects of the wedding – including the church service, associated music, flowers, decorations and reception – will be paid for by the groom's father, the Prince of Wales. The Duke of Cambridge, Prince William, was always expected to be Harry's best man, or "supporter". When an interviewer asked about the possibility of him being best man, William responded: "He hasn't asked me yet." He then added, with a laugh, "So, it could be a sensitive issue."

Harry's nephew and niece Prince George and Princess Charlotte will be among the page boys and flower girls. The ceremony will be conducted by the Dean of Windsor, the Rt Revd. David Conner. Officiating as the couple take their marriage vows will be the Archbishop of Canterbury, The Most Revd. and Rt Hon. Justin Welby. He also baptised Meghan into the Church of England a few months before the wedding day, describing it as "beautiful, sincere and very moving". Archbishop Welby jokingly disclosed that his biggest concerns ahead of the Royal Wedding was dropping the rings and forgetting the vows.

"

From flowers to seating plans, the happy couple will be looking to take charge of their ceremony

"

Opposite: Prince Harry's niece and nephew, Princess Charlotte and Prince George, will be among the flower girls and page boys

Overleaf: Royal weddings, such as that of Prince William and Catherine Middleton in 2011, have grown to become truly global celebrations

The Archbishop has formed a close bond with the engaged couple as they have readied themselves for the big day. In an interview before the ceremony, he said: "You know, at the heart of it are two people who have fallen in love with each other, who are committing their lives to each other with the most beautiful words and profound thoughts, who do it in the presence of God." He added: "You just focus on the couple. It's their day."

In February, Mel B, one of the Spice Girls, gave a big hint that all five members of the all-girl band – Melanie Brown, Melanie Chisholm, Emma Bunton, Geri Horner née Halliwell and Victoria Beckham – would reunite for the Royal Wedding, confirming that they were to attend. The singer claimed she had received a "proper" invitation during an appearance on a television chat show. Sir Elton John has reportedly cancelled two of the dates of his long-standing Las Vegas residency to attend the Royal Wedding, amid speculation he could also be performing.

It promises to be a day of love and celebration, but it's likely that the couple will quickly disappear from the public gaze in the weeks after the wedding. Following the carriage ride around Windsor and all the public adulation, the happy couple are likely to ride back into Windsor Castle and step into St George's Hall – the venue for royal weddings for centuries, notably that of the Prince of Wales and the Duchess of Cornwall in 2005 – for the first of two receptions.

For their wedding cake, Harry and Meghan chose the pastry chef Claire Ptak, owner of the Violet Bakery in Hackney, east London, to create a lemon elderflower cake to incorporate the bright flavours of spring. Covered with buttercream and decorated with fresh flowers it will be a work of art. "I can't tell you how delighted I am to be chosen to make Prince Harry and Ms Markle's wedding cake," said Claire. "Knowing that they really share the same values as I do about food provenance, sustainability, seasonality and – most importantly – flavour, makes this the most exciting event to be a part of." Meghan had previously interviewed the California-raised Ptak for her former lifestyle website TheTig.com, where she celebrated food and travel, and featured interviews with friends and role models to discuss philanthropy and community.

A GLOBAL CELEBRATION

As the role of the British Royal Family has evolved to be more symbolic, so royal weddings have followed suit. In the past, prior to the late 19th century, such unions were relatively low-key affairs that consummated alliances between countries and kingdoms. This begun to change under Queen Victoria's reign, when the royal weddings of her children and grandchildren started to become extravagant affairs attracting big crowds that filled the streets. But it was not until the age of television that the vast pulling power of royal weddings emerged.

The wedding of Harry's father and mother, Prince Charles and Lady Diana Spencer, was watched by a global audience of 750 million people, a sixth of the world's population, in 1981. The global audience exceeded well over a billion souls when his brother Prince William married Catherine in 2011. Harry and Meghan's wedding is also expected to attract huge viewing figures, especially with Meghan being an American. As the brilliant Victorian essayist, journalist and constitutional expert Walter Bagehot wrote years ago, "a princely marriage is the brilliant edition of a universal fact, and, as such, it rivets mankind".

Bagehot is right. This amazing spectacle will not only be Harry and Meghan's wedding, it will be embraced by all those watching. And those who celebrate – either by attending, by cheering on the streets of Windsor or by watching on television – will be delighted to be a part of it too.

Chapter Two

THE ENGAGEMENT

Following the official announcement
of Harry and Meghan's engagement in
November 2017, a picture soon emerged
of a happy and down-to-earth young
couple, who are clearly besotted
with each other

The announcement came in that most modern of ways – via an official statement from the Prince of Wales's office, Clarence House, issued via Twitter. The loving couple, Harry and Meghan, may only have been dating since the summer of 2016 but it came as no surprise, with media commentators predicting that this 16-month romance would result in marriage.

The official statement, issued on 27 November 2017, read: "His Royal Highness The Prince of Wales is delighted to announce the engagement of Prince Harry to Ms Meghan Markle. The wedding will take place in spring 2018. Further details about the wedding day will be announced in due course. His Royal Highness and Ms Markle became engaged in London earlier this month. Prince Harry has informed Her Majesty The Queen and other close members of his family. Prince Harry has also sought and received the blessing of Ms Markle's parents. The couple will live in Nottingham Cottage at Kensington Palace."

This was quickly followed by statements from the Queen and Prince Harry's brother Prince William. The Queen and the Duke of Edinburgh said they were "delighted" for their grandson and his bride-to-be, and "wish them every happiness". "We are very excited for Harry and Meghan," said the Duke and Duchess of Cambridge. "It has been wonderful getting to know Meghan and to see how happy she and Harry are together." Ms Markle's parents wished their daughter and Harry "a lifetime of happiness", adding that they were "incredibly happy" for Meghan and Harry.

"Our daughter has always been a kind and loving person. To see her union with Harry, who shares the same qualities, is a source of great joy for us as parents." Visiting Poundbury in Dorset, the Prince of Wales said he was "thrilled" and "very happy indeed" for Prince Harry and Meghan.

A FIRST APPEARANCE

A few hours after the official announcement, the beaming couple made a public appearance together, carefully choreographed by the army of Buckingham Palace press officers, in the Sunken Garden at Kensington Palace. The location was chosen by Harry in a sentimental nod to his late mother, Princess Diana, who would often visit the garden seeking moments of contemplation as she admired the floral displays as they changed through spring and summer during her all too short lifetime.

Meghan, hand in hand with her prince, looked stunning in a white coat, produced by the Canadian brand Line the Label, and her dress by Italian designer Paolo Rossello's label P.A.R.O.S.H. The "Meghan effect" was already underway, it would appear, with Line the Label's website crashing shortly afterwards due to the number of people trying to access it. Her shoes, strappy Aquazzura Matilde Crisscross Nude Suede Pumps, proved just as popular. The royal bride-to-be then proudly showed off her three-stone diamond engagement ring, designed by Harry himself. It included two diamonds from the personal collection of Princess Diana, as well as a diamond from Botswana, where the couple vacationed to celebrate Meghan's 36th birthday. The band was made of gold and the ring was made by Cleave and Company, court jewellers and medallists to the Queen.

The couple braved the biting November cold to answer a number of questions from the waiting press, who were strategically separated from them by several metres of water. Harry and Meghan stood on

"
As a matter of fact,
I could barely let you
finish proposing, I said,
'Can I say yes now?'
"

the other side of the large ornamental pond before waving at the cameras and walking back through the garden, arm in arm.

Meghan is the first American to marry into the British Royal Family since Wallis Simpson, a twice divorced American socialite from Baltimore whose marriage to Edward VIII led to his abdication. However, it was a very different world back then, when divorce was regarded as unacceptable in society.

Meghan said that she was "so very happy, thank you" to be engaged to Harry. The Prince said he was "thrilled, over the moon" adding: "Very glad it's not raining, as well." They smiled and giggled throughout their appearance. When Harry was asked how he proposed, Ms Markle replied "Save that", with Harry adding: "That will come later." Answering questions posed by waiting journalists, the Prince laughed as he declared he knew his girlfriend was the one "the very first time we met", before they left with their arms around each other and heads affectionately close together.

THE INTERVIEW

In a 20-minute interview following their engagement announcement, the Prince and Meghan shared intimate details of their hopes – from having a family to setting off around the Commonwealth to carve out their joint future as working royals. Still giggling, they sat down in Kensington Palace for an interview with the BBC's Mishal Husain, revealing how they fell in love and conducted their long-distance love affair across the Atlantic.

"The fact that I fell in love with Meghan so incredible quickly was confirmation to me that all the stars have aligned and everything was just perfect," said a gushing Harry. It started, he said, with a blind date and they eventually fell in love under the stars in Botswana. He joked that when, on a meeting with

the Queen, her notoriously snappy corgis gave Meghan their seal of approval, he knew a royal wedding was inevitable.

Meghan revealed that Harry had proposed over a chicken dinner conducted in their "cosy" cottage. The couple, who saw each other every two weeks during the early stages of their relationship, disclosed how the Royal Family helped their relationship blossom, with the "incredible" Queen and "fantastically supportive" Duchess of Cambridge helping her settle in.

"This beautiful woman just tripped and fell into my life," said Harry. "We're a fantastic team, we know we are and over time we hope to have as much impact as possible." Set up by a mutual female friend, whom the couple declined to name, the Prince and a then-stranger were persuaded onto a blind date. Meghan, who claimed to know little about the Royal Family, asked nothing of the man she was being set up with, other than, "is he nice?"

"Because I'm from the States you don't grow up with the same understanding of the Royal Family," she said. "And so, while I now understand very clearly there is a global interest there, I didn't know much about him and so the only thing that I had asked her when she said she wanted to set us up was, 'Well, is he nice?' Because if he wasn't kind it just didn't seem like it would make sense."

Harry, too, knew little about his blind date, having never watched the television show *Suits* that Meghan starred in. "I'd never even heard of her," he said. "I was beautifully surprised when I walked into that room and saw her sitting there. I was like, wow, I really have done well, I've got to up my game."

After one date, Harry immediately asked to see her again the following day. "And then it was like, right,

diaries," he said. "We need to get the diaries out and find out how we're going to make this work, because I was off to Africa for a month, she was working. And we just said right where's the gap? And the gap happened to be in the perfect place."

From then on, their love blossomed. They spent time with "cosy nights in in front of the television, cooking dinner in our little cottage", said Harry. "It's made us a hell of a lot closer in a short space of time. For us, it's an opportunity for really getting to know each other without people looking or trying to take photos on their phones."

While hidden away in Nottingham Cottage, they spent time with William and Catherine, as well as taking tea with the Prince of Wales and the Queen. "William was longing to meet her and so was Catherine, so, you know, being our neighbours we managed to get that in quite a few times," said Harry. "Catherine has been absolutely amazing, as has William as well, you know, fantastic support."

"Just to take the time to be able to go on long country walks and just talk," said Meghan, who said the relationship had not felt like a whirlwind to them. "I think we were able to really have so much time just to connect and we never went longer than two weeks without seeing each other, even though we were obviously doing a long-distance relationship. So we made it work."

THE PROPOSAL

Harry's proposal came after an evening of domestic bliss. "Just a cosy night," said Meghan, in which they were "trying" to roast a chicken. "It was just an amazing surprise, it was so sweet and natural and very romantic. He got on one knee."

"

The fact that I fell in love with Meghan so incredibly quickly was confirmation to me that all the stars have aligned

"

Asked whether she had said "yes" immediately, she told the Prince: "As a matter of fact, I could barely let you finish proposing, I said, 'Can I say yes now?'"

Harry confirmed this. "She didn't even let me finish. She said, 'can I say yes, can I say yes?' and then there were hugs. I had the ring in my finger and I was like 'can I give you the ring?' She goes 'oh yes, the ring'. So, no it was a really nice moment, it was just the two of us and I think I managed to catch her by surprise as well."

FAMILY SUPPORT

As this was before the birth of the Duke and Duchess of Cambridge's third child and Harry was fifth in line to the throne at the time, Her Majesty The Queen had to give her formal blessing for the marriage to take place. Harry said she was "delighted" and the Prince of Wales invited Meghan for tea. Harry's aunts on the Spencer side, to whom he has remained close, also spent time with the happy couple.

Harry expressed his surprise that his girlfriend was able to win over the Queen's corgis when she met his grandmother. He revealed that the normally snappy dogs sat happily at her feet during tea. "The corgis took to you straight away," said Harry. "I've spent the last 33 years being barked at; this one walks in, absolutely nothing. Just wagging tails and I was just like 'argh'."

Meghan said she had met the Queen several times and said it was "incredible" to get to know her through her grandson's eyes. "It's incredible to be able to meet her through his lens," she said, "not just with his honour and respect for her as the monarch, but the love that he has for her as his grandmother. All of those layers have been so important for me, so that when I met her I had such a deep understanding and, of course, incredible respect for being able to have that time with her. She's an incredible woman."

Harry added: "The family together have been absolutely a solid support. My grandparents, as well, have been wonderful throughout this whole process and they've known for quite some time. So how they haven't told anybody is again a miracle in itself. But now the whole family have come together and have been a huge amount of support."

The Prince also told of his meetings with his future mother-in-law, saying she was "amazing". He is yet to meet Ms Markle's father, Thomas, but has spoken to him on the telephone and did ask for permission to marry his daughter.

As a mixed-race woman, Ms Markle said, she had found some of the reaction to her ethnicity "disheartening". "It's a shame that that is the climate in this world to focus on a matter that's discriminatory," she said. "But I think, at the end of the day, I'm really just proud of who I am and where I come from." Her parents and close friends, she said, were a little concerned by her new-found public image, but were quickly won over after realising "they also had never seen me so happy".

"I know that I'm in love with this girl and I hope that she's in love with me," Prince Harry said, of the moment he realised she would be taking on a "media storm". "But we still had to sit down on the sofa and have some pretty frank conversations to say, 'what you're letting yourself in for is a big deal and it's not easy for anybody'. At the end of the day, she chooses me and I choose her and, whatever we have to tackle, it will be us together as a team. She's capable of anything and together there's a hell of a lot of work that needs doing.

"The fact that I know she will be unbelievably good at the job part of it as well is obviously a huge relief to me," continued Harry. "For me, it's an added member of the family. It's another team player as part of the bigger team. Both of us have passions for wanting to make change for good. With lots of young people running around the Commonwealth, that's where we want to spend most of our time. There's a lot to do."

Chapter Three

THE SECRET ROMANCE

—————

Harry and Meghan managed to keep their relationship under wraps for six months before the official announcement that put the couple well and truly in the spotlight

Conducting a relationship with a celebrity can be a complicated business. There are the red carpets to negotiate, the ever-present, persistent paparazzi snapping away at any given minute, plus all those loaded questions in interviews to talk around. But somehow, one of the most famous and eligible men on the planet managed to keep his relationship secret for nearly half a year before the news broke.

Meghan Markle, who starred as para-legal Rachel Zane in the popular television drama series *Suits*, was first rumoured to be dating Prince Harry in October 2016, when reports claimed they had been seeing each other since July. They had, in fact, met while Harry was promoting the Invictus Games – the event he had launched for disabled military personnel – in London and Meghan shared a picture of herself visiting Buckingham Palace on 5 July. She had also been spotted in the Royal Box at the Wimbledon tennis tournament on 28 June and 4 July, leading to speculation that she was already well acquainted with Harry's family. As it turned out, both reports were true because Meghan and Harry had actually started dating long before the news leaked out, as she revealed in the October cover interview with the popular culture and current affairs magazine, *Vanity Fair*, entitled, "Meghan Markle, Wild About Harry!"

"We were very quietly dating for about six months before it became news, and I was working during that

whole time, and the only thing that changed was people's
perception," she told Vanity Fair writer Sam Kushner.
"Nothing about me changed. I'm still the same person that
I am, and I've never defined myself by my relationship."

In fact, the relationship had moved relatively slowly
at first and the couple had taken every precaution to keep
it under wraps. Meghan even had a code name she used
for the Prince when she was on set.

A STATEMENT OF INTENT

It was actually Harry himself who transformed their
discreet intimacy into a full-blown public royal romance.
Whether it was his intention or not, his statement – meant
as an impassioned demand for their privacy to be respected –
meant the couple were even more under the spotlight as
he had confirmed Meghan as his "girlfriend" and that they
were serious about each other.

It was a bold move. Purporting to be from his press
secretary, the unflappable Jason Knauf, it was an
unprecedented press release, deeply personal in style,
suggesting that it had been dictated by Harry himself,
coming straight from the heart. Harry, known for his
fiery temperament, pulled no punches. He attacked the
excesses of some elements of the press over what he
interpreted to be a "wave of abuse". He utterly condemned
what he described as "racial undertones" directed at

"

One of the most famous and eligible men on the planet managed to keep his relationship secret for nearly half a year before the news broke

"

Left: The couple are relishing their royal duties, but have also savoured time away from the glare of public attention

Meghan in media reports. He was also clear, in a nod to what happened to his late mother, Diana, Princess of Wales, that he feared for the safety of his girlfriend and her family and gallantly wanted to protect them all.

Harry believed that "a line has been crossed" in the excessive reporting of his private life, which he regarded as a gross intrusion. Harry claimed he had never before witnessed such a "degree of pressure, scrutiny and harassment" from the media. He also complained about a "smear on the front page" of one newspaper about Ms Markle and that her lawyers were engaged in "nightly legal battles to keep defamatory stories out of papers". Palace sources added that police had had to be called after a photographer allegedly barged into the actress's garage in Toronto.

What particularly shocked the defensive prince was the "dangerous relationship" in which newspaper reports and comment pieces that he considered "racist and sexist" sparked a torrent of vitriol against Markle on Twitter and other social media platforms, as well as in comment sections below online news stories. Markle's father, Thomas, is white and her mother, Doria Ragland, African-American, and Meghan had written about her heritage on her website, describing herself as biracial and "half black and half white", which has been referenced in many articles about Harry's new relationship.

PROTECTIVE INSTINCTS

Harry was understood to have been particularly irritated with one commentary by columnist Rachel Johnson, sister of the British Foreign Secretary Boris Johnson, and its "racist" tone. It read that, if the couple had children, "The Windsors will thicken their watery, thin blue blood and Spencer pale skin and ginger hair with some rich and exotic DNA".

The Palace statement also complained of the "bombardment of nearly every friend, co-worker, and loved one in her life" and the harassment of her mother at her home in Los Angeles, who has had to "struggle past photographers in order to get to her front door". "Given what she was going through in the press and what was happening privately, Harry no longer felt it was acceptable for someone in his position to sit quietly," a Palace source said.

Harry, who lived with the horror of how his mother was – in his view – hounded to her death by relentless paparazzo, was not prepared to sit around and watch them destroy Meghan and his life too. But this action was happening because of him, not her. Meghan, who had lived and revelled in media attention for years, was apparently fairly relaxed. But for Harry, the grin-and-say-nothing policy was not going to wash.

He was not naive; Harry knew that the media attention would continue, but he wanted to lay down a marker and he wanted the people who were lapping up these stories to at least know what he felt about them. The Prince was also concerned that the press would consider that any girl he has a relationship with may be "the one" and would be treated as fair game.

"That is a very difficult place for any woman to be in, and being in a position where he is not able to protect her is a very serious concern for him," the source added.

Prince Harry had acted decisively. His two previous serious relationships, with Chelsy Davy and Cressida Bonas, had faltered under the strain of media attention and he did not want history to repeat itself. By the middle of 2016, he had been single for a couple of years, although during interviews he had spoken of his desire to settle down and start a family once he found the right woman.

By the time he calmly sat down with Meghan for their engagement interview 12 months later, he was much more sanguine. When Meghan admitted her experience as Harry's girlfriend had been a learning curve and she did not have any understanding of just what it would be like, Harry jumped in. "I tried to warn you as much as possible, but I think both of us were

totally surprised by the reaction. I think you can have as many conversation as you want and try and prepare as much as possible, but we were totally unprepared for what happened after that."

GOING PUBLIC

In fact, if anything, the attention strengthened their relationship. Once they had gone public, Meghan was happy to speak openly and warmly of their love. She spoke of Harry as her "boyfriend" in the *Vanity Fair* interview and was gushing about their intimacy. In the clearest signal that this royal romance would end in marriage, she said, brazenly, "We're a couple. We're in love." There could be no going back now.

"I'm sure there will be a time when we will have to come forward and present ourselves and have stories to tell, but I hope what people will understand is that this is our time," she went on. "This is for us. It is part of what makes it so special, that it's just ours. But we're happy. Personally, I love a great love story. I can tell you that at the end of the day I think it's really simple. We're two people who are really happy and in love."

Chapter Four

"HI, I'M MEGHAN"

Harry and Meghan followed the
announcement of their engagement
with a nationwide meet-and-greet tour,
introducing the glamorous bride-to-be
to well-wishers throughout the
United Kingdom

After more than a year of preserving their privacy, the prince and his US actress girlfriend decided to take their relationship to the next level by going public. The moment came with their first ever joint public appearance at the third Invictus Games, the international multi-sport event that Prince Harry created for wounded, injured or sick armed services personnel. Harry launched the games in London in March 2014, took them to Florida in May 2016, and then to Toronto in September 2017.

At the opening ceremony for the Toronto games, Meghan may have sat separately from Harry under the watchful eye of a protection officer but it was a significant sign of how serious their relationship was. Later in the week, they attended the tennis together in a surprise appearance in front of the cameras. The cat was now well and truly out of the bag.

By the time the Invictus Games had come to an end the couple were happy to go public. They were not shy around each other. They joined Meghan's mother, Doria Ragland, in a suite at the Air Canada Centre for the closing ceremony. They were reportedly "snuggling, kissing, with their arms around each other".

Harry reportedly left his official seat after the ceremony began and went to the seats occupied by Meghan, Doria, Jessica Mulroney (daughter-in-law of the former Canadian Prime Minister Brian Mulroney) and Markus Anderson (the Canadian who introduced

Meghan and Harry). Meghan even wore a white shirt, made by the American fashion designer Misha Nonoo, called "The Husband" – a name that got the media tongues wagging. Perhaps, the travelling press pack concluded, an announcement of a royal wedding wasn't that far off.

Harry chatted openly about his girlfriend, as well. He said that Meghan Markle was "loving" the Invictus Games after she attended the wheelchair tennis hand-in-hand with him. It was the first time that Prince Harry had spoken publicly and freely about Meghan, following the written statement released by Kensington Palace that confirmed their relationship. As far as the press were concerned the countdown to the royal wedding had started. They were not wrong.

THE ANNOUNCEMENT

A series of stories followed. Meghan giving up her social media platforms, talk of her negotiating her exit from the hugely successful drama *Suits*, stories of romantic holidays in Norway and Botswana, and her attendance at the wedding of the Duchess of Cambridge's sister, Pippa Middleton, all stoked the rumour fire.

Then it emerged that Harry had taken his girlfriend to formally meet the Queen at the Palace to get her blessing for the marriage, something he was obliged to ask for under the Succession to the Crown Act 2013. Her Majesty gave her permission willingly, thrilled that at last her grandson, with whom she is very close, had found the one he could share his life with.

Finally, after another weekend of frenzied media speculation, the official announcement came from Clarence House, Prince Charles's office, on Monday 27 November.

It did not come as any surprise to the media or the public, but what did was the speed with which this royal bride-to-be would get to work. Within days she was on her way to Nottingham with Harry at her side for the first of several trips around the UK to familiarise herself with the country that would be her new home. Within a few months of the engagement announcement, Harry and Meghan had toured around the United Kingdom, visiting every country in the Queen's realm, taking in Nottingham, Brixton in south London, Edinburgh, Cardiff and Belfast.

It was quite an education for the Californian actress, meeting thousands of people, shaking thousands of hands and making small talk with complete strangers, but she took it in her stride. Often not waiting for Harry to show her the way, she would introduce herself with a cheery "Hi, I'm Meghan." As she worked the line of well-wishers behind the steel security barriers during a walkabout she would add, "I'm so happy, it's just such a thrill to be here."

"

It was quite an education for the Californian actress, shaking thousands of hands and making small talk with complete strangers, but she took it in her stride

"

Below: Meghan was touched by the rapturous welcome she received in south London when she and Harry visited a local radio station

A WARM RECEPTION

On her first public outing, to the city of Nottingham, the public waited patiently in freezing winter conditions from 6am to meet the newly engaged couple. Many were clutching gifts, flowers and homemade cards. Meghan made a beeline for children, who seemed thrilled to meet her, accepting congratulations from them and showing off her engagement ring. Her first official gift came from Ian Curryer, chief executive of Nottingham City Council, who gave her and the prince a silver pin in the shape of Robin Hood – Nottinghamshire's legendary outlaw depicted in folklore, literature and film – with a bow and arrow, in honour of what they had done for the local area. Harry told him he was "delighted to be here" adding, "Look at the number of people here, isn't it great!"

Waving to people in the windows above the narrow street, Meghan walked down a line asking people their names, where they are from and endearingly introducing herself. She seemed to have no problem with the limelight.

One ardent and proud royalist, Irene Hardman, of the nearby Nottinghamshire village of Ruddington, made sure she knew it wasn't all about Meghan and celebrity, however. Royalty is different, she insisted. Irene, 81, had been handing Harry a bag of his favourite sweets, Haribos, every time he had visited the city. This time, she bought the happy couple a bag of goodies, including a copy of the local newspaper, the *Nottingham Post*. "I told her: 'Look after him for us'. She said she would," said an emotional Irene. "I cried – I think she's wonderful, and it's fantastic. They're so genuine."

After the walkabout, Prince Harry and Ms Markle went to the Nottingham Contemporary Exhibition Centre for an

event to mark World Aids Day. Dominic Edwards, from the
Terrence Higgins Trust, a charity supported by Harry's late
mother Princess Diana, said the charity was "thrilled" the
couple had chosen to visit Nottingham and the Terrence
Higgins Trust event. "I think it really underlines his great
support for HIV as a cause."

THE TOUR CONTINUES

The couples' next stop a few days later was multicultural
Brixton in south London, where they met presenters at
Reprezent 107.3 FM – the only UK radio station presented
solely by young people. They listened intently as they were
told how the station trains hundreds of young people each
year in media and employment skills. As they arrived, fans
began chanting, "I love you Meghan." The small crowd
didn't even shout for Harry, something he would have to
get used to. She seemed overwhelmed when she got out
the car and kept turning towards the crowd causing a
hysterical reaction. Harry tapped her on her shoulder to
advise her to turn away.

 Inside, fittingly, the pair listened to the track "Flirt"
by the artist Poté and Meghan praised teenage presenter
Gloria Beyi, 17, telling her: "I can see why your show is
so popular. You're so thoughtful and your approach is
so engaging." Harry told the station's founder, Shane
Carey, 46, the work he was doing was "amazing", while
Meghan made everyone laugh when she told them:
"I must tune in."

 Afterwards, they greeted well-wishers who had
waited for hours in the freezing cold and even stopped to
pose for selfies. Foster carer Sharley Watson, 55, waited

out in the cold for hours to catch a glimpse of the couple and said she was excited to welcome them to Brixton. "It's good to see Meghan in Brixton, a black community," said Sharley. "It's the first time we've had a royal visit here. Hopefully she will want to help areas like this. I hope she liked it."

WELCOME TO WALES

Dressed in a stylish black coat, Meghan won over the principality of Wales when she visited Cardiff with Harry in January. She signed autographs, was given flowers, had her hand kissed – and even took part in a group hug, passing her initiation with flying colours.

Inside the castle, Cardiff's landmark building with a history that dates back over 1,000 years, the couple toured a Welsh culture festival. They heard performances from musicians and poets, met leading sportsmen and women, and saw how organisations were working to promote the Welsh language and cultural identity.

It was all a learning curve for Meghan, who broke royal protocol when she signed an autograph for Caitlin Clark, 10 – signing: "Hi Kaitlin" – albeit with a K – and adding a heart and a smiley face. The schoolgirl was overjoyed. "My heart is still racing," she said, "I've never got a royal autograph before. This is going to make everyone jealous."

She was lauded by Jessica Phillips, 23, for her outspoken feminist views. Meghan replied: "He [Harry] is a feminist too, so there's that." Freelance journalist Phillips said afterwards: "She was so lovely. I said it was really lovely to have a feminist in the Royal Family and she said Harry is a feminist too."

In February, they headed north to Scotland's capital, Edinburgh, for their fourth joint visit. Wrapped up warmly they were greeted by Frank Ross, Edinburgh's Lord Lieutenant and Lord Provost. Large crowds had gathered on the castle's esplanade, where the Royal Edinburgh Military Tattoo is staged every year.

Meghan, stylish in a Burberry coat and Veronica Beard trousers, enjoyed one moment in particular when a mischievous military mascot Corporal Cruachan IV – a Shetland pony – proved too much to handle. Cruachan, who once famously nibbled a posy being held by the Queen, greeted Meghan with a curious sniff. Sensibly, she decided to keep her distance, but when Harry gave him a pat he was rewarded with an attempted nip.

At the castle, Harry and Meghan joined Sergeant Dave Beveridge for the firing of the One O'Clock Gun. They were given ear defenders before standing behind the gun, which dates back to 1861. They also chatted to cadets and took in views across the city, before briefly waving to the adoring crowds as they departed.

Chapter Five

THE FAB FOUR

Together with William and Kate, Harry
and Meghan make up an impressive
foursome – and a fine ambassadorial
team for their Royal Foundation

The Windsors, the world's most-watched family, have more rules and traditions than most. If you're in a room with the Queen and Her Majesty stands up, it is protocol for everyone to follow suit. When dining as a family, after the Queen has taken her last bite, everyone else at the table needs to stop eating, too. Men of the Royal Family perform a neck bow, while women curtsy when greeting the Queen for the first time during the day. And every royal bride, including Meghan, carries myrtle in her wedding bouquet.

But perhaps the most important rule, and one that has implications for the survival of this ancient and unelected institution, is that the Royal Family is not allowed to vote, hold any type of political office or speak publicly about politics. They must certainly not be seen to be partisan, supporting one political party or another, as to do so could cause a constitutional crisis.

Meghan, an outspoken feminist and campaigner in her past, used her celebrity status in the 2016 US Presidential Election to endorse Hillary Clinton and criticise the eventual victor, Donald Trump, as "misogynistic" and "divisive". But that was in her past. Such strident opinions will have to be muted as she embraces her life as a member of the British Royal Family. Instead, she will be expected to channel her campaigning zeal into relatively non-political or apolitical roles, such as supporting the voluntary sector.

However, Meghan is a mature woman with a voice and she is clearly not afraid to use it. It appears that she will not easily be silenced by the niceties of royal protocol.

In February, during the inaugural Royal Foundation Forum, she spoke about a variety of topics at the "Making a Difference Together" event – including her support for women's empowerment movements like Time's Up and #MeToo – but at the same time demonstrating the bond she has formed with her future family.

It was her first official appearance alongside Harry, Prince William and Kate, and Meghan appeared to perfectly complement the experienced royal trio. "Togetherness at its finest," she said of the two couples' relationship with each other. The press duly dubbed the two couples "the Fab Four".

There was a special significance to the four of them appearing on stage together. The Royal Foundation was a charity begun by Princes William and Harry in 2009 and later supported by the Duchess of Cambridge. Under its umbrella sit a variety of charities, including the Heads Together mental health campaign, the Invictus Games for ex-service personnel, a cyberbullying taskforce, and assorted initiatives on the environment, education, employment training and addiction.

Meghan must have been fully briefed about what was expected of her in her future role as Harry's wife.

But what was interesting about Meghan's first speaking role on her royal journey was her supreme confidence to speak her mind. She signalled her support for global movements aimed at ending sexual harassment, in a stroke suggesting that the younger generation of the Royal Family could harness their momentum to highlight the issue of women's empowerment. She added that there was "no better time" to continue to raise the profile of women's voices.

FUTURE VISION

In a public Q&A session, all four were invited to lay out their plans for the future. "You'll often hear people say, 'you're helping women find their voices'," she said of her work as a campaigner. "I fundamentally disagree with that because women don't need to find a voice: they have a voice. They need to feel empowered to use it and people need to be encouraged to listen.

"I think right now, in the climate we are seeing, so many campaigns – I mean Me Too and Time's Up – there is no better time than now to really continue to shine a light on women feeling empowered and people really helping to support them, men included in that. It makes such a tremendous difference."

Making a small concession to her wedding planning at the prompting of Harry, she added: "So I guess we

"

Meghan is a mature woman with a voice and she is clearly not afraid to use it

"

wait a couple of months and then we can hit the ground running. We can multitask, that's fine!"

The foursome also poked fun at the perils of working together. "Working as a family does have its challenges, of course it does," Prince Harry said, to laughter. "We're stuck together forever now!"

Meghan said they each brought their own perspectives to issues. "If everyone's thinking the same way," she said, "how are you going to push the envelope, how are you really going to break through in a different sort of mindset?" It was an accomplished performance from an accomplished actress.

PUBLIC AFFECTION

A few days later, Harry and Meghan were on the road again. In Birmingham in early March they seemed much more at ease working together in public. They appeared to be getting the hang of it.

They were very tactile publicly, much more than William and Kate ever are. While Harry and Meghan had previously been seen holding hands and grasping arms, on this "away-day" visit to the Midlands they displayed more intimate gestures, playful pats and

Previous pages and below: Harry and Meghan have not been afraid to show public displays of affection, as they did on their visit to Birmingham earlier in the year

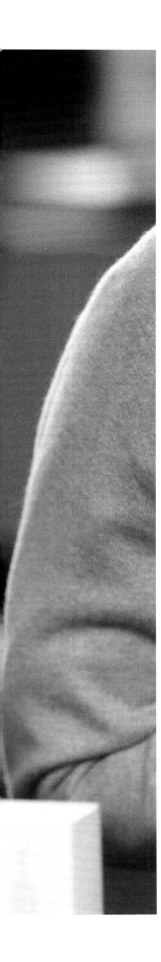

hands on the smalls of each other's backs. It was as if they were almost oblivious to the crowds around them. This newfound confidence was reflected in the way they interacted with the crowd too. Schoolgirl Sophia Richards, 10, got closer than most to Meghan after she was swept into an impromptu embrace with the future royal.

The couple were there to celebrate the aspirations of young women on International Women's Day and, despite enduring a wait in the drizzling rain, enthusiastic locals cheered and waved Union Flags as they finally caught sight of the royal pair, who stopped to speak to onlookers as they made their way to Millennium Point. Meghan – dressed in a coat by J.Crew, trousers by Alexander Wang and an AllSaints jumper – was greeted by shouts of "You're beautiful!"

While in the city, they attended an event encouraging young women to pursue careers in science, technology, engineering and maths (STEM). Hosted by social enterprise "Stemettes", the event saw the couple speak to students about the challenges of working in male-dominated STEM industries.

The pair donned headsets resembling a virtual-reality rollercoaster. Meghan said she was shocked by some of the technology on display, including pianos made out of bananas and how to "hack the web". She told some students that the coding they were working on looked very impressive, saying: "Wow, that's really cool."

FAMILY PLANS?

On their fifth away-day – an unannounced visit to Northern Ireland – Meghan dropped a huge baby hint. She made it clear that she and Harry are already thinking about starting a family during a visit to a science park. She gestured at an array of baby equipment and said: "I am sure at one point we will need the whole thing."

The couple were eager to find out about the latest products for new parents and their infants when they were shown items produced by Shnuggle, a firm that makes innovative baby products, including a baby bath that enables the baby to sit up, a changing mat and a Moses basket.

"It's very sweet," said Meghan. Sinead Murphy, who founded the company with her husband Adam, said: "They seemed very engaged with the products. Harry was particularly interested in the bath. I wonder if he has witnessed bath time with his nephew or niece. As soon as he saw the bum bump [which stops the baby slipping down] he understood immediately. He said, 'Oh, non-slip'."

Asked to interpret Meghan's baby hint, she said: "With an upcoming marriage it's likely there is going to be an announcement in the next few years."

Harry himself dropped a big hint in November during the engagement interview that babies will be on the horizon soon. When asked, "Children?" Harry replied drily: "Not currently no," and then added: "One step at a time and hopefully we'll start a family in the near future."

Chapter Six

THE FUTURE

One of Harry and Meghan's main roles in
the future is likely to be as "super envoys"
for the Commonwealth, continuing the
invaluable service the Queen has done
for more than 60 years

At the opening ceremony for the Toronto games, she enthusiastically sang the words to the national anthem "God Save The Queen" in the highly significant Westminster Abbey service. Meghan may have grown up an American, unaware of the significance of the Commonwealth, but it is clear that this international institution will play a huge role in the rest of her life.

As she sat next to her fiancé and among all the senior royals for the annual Commonwealth Day service at Westminster Abbey, the importance of her new role must have dawned on her. Harry had declared the service in March was a "pretty special occasion".

Meghan only had to look at the beaming smile on the face of her fiancé's grandmother – the head of the institution and thus a matriarchal figure to a third of the world's population – to gauge what it meant to the 91-year-old monarch.

At the age of 21, the Queen had publicly dedicated herself to the service of the Commonwealth and its people. Now she was ready to pass that baton of responsibility to her son, Prince Charles, and to her wider family.

Her Majesty clearly cherishes the Commonwealth. The institution – an intergovernmental organisation of 53 independent states, most of them former British colonies – was formally constituted in 1949 and has been strengthened since she became its head in 1953. It will be the Queen's legacy and she expects the next generation

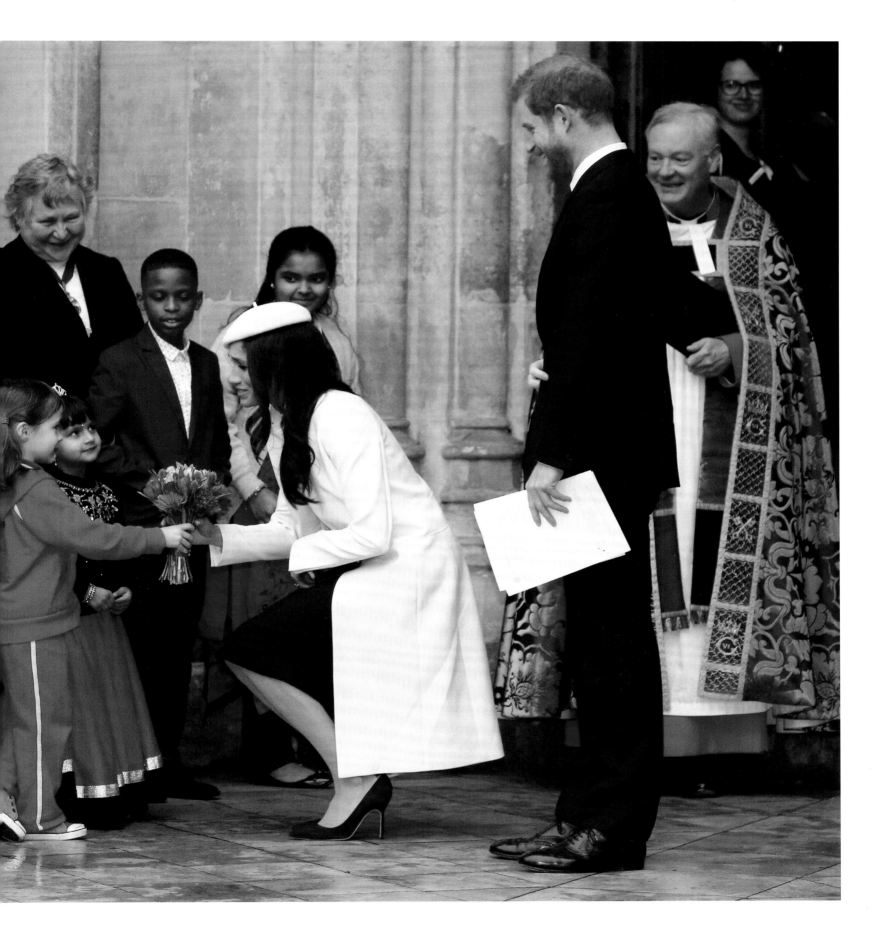

of royals – including Meghan – to understand it and serve it with equal dedication. Harry and Meghan had already spoken of their passion for the Commonwealth cause, using their engagement interview to spell out their hopes for engaging with its young people.

A FINE PERFORMANCE

If Meghan looked a little nervous at first it was understandable. After being invited to join the Queen at one of the most important events of her year, she was keen to make a good impression. The former actress, who has undertaken to become a British citizen, appeared to have been doing some research ahead of her first official engagement alongside Her Majesty, a major milestone for the bride-to-be.

She confidently joined in with the national anthem, paying respect to her future grandmother-in-law, faultlessly singing "God Save The Queen" and two hymns, "Lord Of All Hopefulness" and "Guide Me, O Thou Great Redeemer" with gusto.

The service saw the Royal Family out in force, with the Prince of Wales, the Duchess of Cornwall, the Duke of York, the Princess Royal and the Countess of Wessex among those supporting the Queen and showing their own enthusiasm for the "Commonwealth connection".

Prince William, Kate, Harry and Meghan arrived at the service – which boasted a 2,000-strong congregation – together, taking prominent seats for the televised spectacle. Wearing a cream dress and coat by Amanda Wakeley and beret by Stephen Jones, Ms Markle was cheered by waiting crowds as she stepped out of her car at Westminster Abbey, joining William and Kate to watch a performance from drummers before stepping inside.

During the service, the Prime Minister, Theresa May, gave a Bible reading, Portsmouth Gospel Choir sang "Bridge Over Troubled Water" and Dr Andrew Bastawrous, an eye surgeon who has turned a smartphone into an examination tool to combat avoidable blindness in developing countries, gave the reflection.

The congregation included major Commonwealth figures including the Prime Minister of Malta Joseph Muscat, Commonwealth Secretary-General Baroness Scotland, high commissioners, ambassadors, senior politicians from across the UK and Commonwealth, faith leaders and more than 800 schoolchildren and young people.

"The service was beautiful," Meghan told a visiting teacher, "especially the choir and the music. It was great to see people from all over the world so well represented at the service." She also admitted that

"

The Commonwealth will be the Queen's legacy and she expects the next generation of royals to understand it and serve it with equal dedication

"

she was "very, very excited" when asked about her fast-approaching wedding.

AN INTERNATIONAL ROLE

During her research into the Royal Family, the importance of events such as the Commonwealth Day service would have been impressed upon her. The Royal Family is, after all, a working family – working for the institution of the monarchy in the service of its people.

It is clear that the Queen, who is always personally debriefed by members of her family after overseas Commonwealth visits they have undertaken on her behalf, plans to use the new royal "power couple" as Commonwealth super envoys.

Following their May wedding, Harry and Meghan are expecting to be set to work on major foreign forays to Canada, Australia and New Zealand in the same year. Another key destination for them to visit is India as well as the Commonwealth nations in Africa, but that is not expected until 2019.

The Queen and the now retired Prince Philip, 96, no longer undertake long-haul travel and Her Majesty wants to capitalise on the popularity of her grandson and his bride to cement ties and help smooth the path for trade deals with key Commonwealth nations.

The couple even made a point of mentioning going around the Commonwealth in their BBC engagement interview. "There's a lot to do," they both agreed. They are expected to add to that a royal tour of other areas of Australia, as well as possibly a trip to neighbouring New Zealand later this year. A Foreign Office source confirmed plans are already in the pipeline.

The royals play a key "soft power" role in helping Britain to negotiate new trade agreements. In trade and diplomatic terms, royal visits pack a formidable soft-power punch. The Queen hosted the Commonwealth Heads of Government Meeting this April in London and Windsor. Again Harry and Meghan played highly visible roles. These will be roles that they will play on the world stage for the rest of their lives.

PUBLISHER

St James's House
298 Regents Park Road
London N3 2SZ

Phone: +44 (0)20 8371 4000
publishing@stjamess.org
www.stjamess.org

Richard Freed, Chief Executive
richard.freed@stjamess.org

Stephen van der Merwe, Managing Director
stephen.vdm@stjamess.org

Richard Golbourne, Sales Director
r.golbourne@stjamess.org

Ben Duffy, Communications Director
ben.duffy@stjamess.org

Stephen Mitchell, Head of Editorial
stephen.mitchell@stjamess.org

Aniela Gil, Senior Designer
aniela.gil@stjamess.org

John Lewis, Deputy Editor
john.lewis@stjamess.org

Text
Robert Jobson

Photography
Nunn Syndication, Getty Images